How to Find the Best Home Business that fits Your Needs

Starting a Business QuickStart Guide

[RS Johnson]

Copyright © 2012 *RS Johnson*

All rights reserved.

Table of Contents

Introduction 5
Chapter 1 | Identify your Business Field 6
   Assess Your Talents 6
   Examine Your Skills 7
   Determine Whether Your Ideas Work as Home-Based Businesses 8
   Determine the Likely Profit 9
Chapter 2| Create a Business Plan 11
   The Marketing Plan 11
   Management Plan 17
   The Financial Plan 18
   A Final Word on your Home Based Work Business Plan 23
Chapter 3| Things to Consider Before You Start a Home Business 25
   What Is My Product? 25
   Who Will Buy It? 26
   Who Is the Competition Home Based Business? .. 27
   Where Are the Buyers? How Can I Find Them? ... 28
   How Much Shall I Charge 28
   Typical Pricing Formula 29

Home Based Business Promotion 31
Conclusion 34

Introduction

The best home-based business is when you start because you are passionate about the work and interested in the process involved, not one you saw in a work-at-home ad or a friend recruiting on social media. Many people find entrepreneurship appealing, but figuring out how to start a business can be so overwhelming that it scares people away. What should you offer for sale? To whom should you sell? How are you going to get customers? If that isn't enough, it seems like a new business trend emerges online every other week. Chatbots, Facebook ads, Instagram influencers, and many other options are available. So what should you concentrate on? What is truly important? Stop overthinking and start working to make your business a reality if you're serious about starting one. Starting a business entails planning, making financial decisions, conducting market research, and learning about never-expected topics. It is very critical to recognize that there is no one-size-fits-all approach to starting a new business. Still, this guide will assist you in organizing your thoughts and ironing out important details so that when you launch your business, you have answered all of the critical startup questions.

Chapter 1 | Identify your Business Field

Starting a home-based processing industry, you to be more flexible in terms of how you spend your time and earn money. However, it is not a quick process, nor is it a guarantee of financial success. It necessitates a long-term commitment as well as a thorough understanding of the work involved.

To build a home-based business with a solid foundation and earning potential, you must invest time and resources to determine the best business for you and develop a plan.

Assess Your Talents

Begin by listing your natural talents or the things you are naturally good at. Your skills are the foundation of any successful business venture, including a home-based one. You must be creative, detail-oriented, a strong communicator, persistent, and a quick learner to start a business.

Your abilities are linked to your personality traits, which play an important role in determining whether you are suited for self-employment. For example, openness to experience, self-reliance, achievement motivation, self-efficacy, and comfort with risk are all characteristics shared by successful business owners.

Be truthful in evaluating your skills and personality to determine whether a home-based business is a right path for you. For example, if you don't think you're cut out for self-employment but still want more flexibility in your work life, look for a job that allows you to work from home.

Examine Your Skills

You are born with talents, but you learn to use them over time.

A creative person, for example, may have exceptional writing, artistic, or design abilities. A naturally detail-oriented person may be able to develop strong accounting or organizational skills.

Running a successful business frequently necessitates the acquisition of new skills, such as marketing or cold-calling. In addition, they will frequently point out where you are best suited to apply your natural talents.

To generate business ideas, combine your talents and skills.

When it comes to starting a business, the skills you've spent time and effort learning are frequently the foundation of great business ideas.

A detail-oriented individual with accounting and organization skills, for example, could start a home-based company as a tax preparer, bookkeeper, business manager, financial consultant, professional home organizer, or virtual assistant.

Combining your talents and skills will enable you to generate a plethora of business ideas. However, some will be jobs that you are uninterested in, while others will necessitate more education or certification than you currently have.

As you brainstorm, you get a sense of which business ideas are a good fit for your personality, skill set, and interests. This will properly allow you to focus your efforts on businesses that you are genuinely interested in pursuing.

Determine Whether Your Ideas Work as Home-Based Businesses

Not all businesses will work well as home-based businesses, and some will fail. Starting a business from home necessitates careful consideration of several factors, including your location, zoning, legal restrictions, licensing, work style, personality, and the needs of your family.

A manufacturing business, for example, cannot be started in a residential neighborhood, and a business that requires a high volume of clients coming and going may not be feasible from a home office. Reduce your list of potential businesses to those that:

- Is it possible to conduct them from a home office rather than a separate workspace?

- Allow for the majority of work to be done from home rather than on-site.

This will provide you with a list of business ideas that are feasible and feasible for you to start from the comfort of your own home.

Determine the Likely Profit

To start a profitable home-based business, you must first consider its potential profitability. You may have a great talent and the skills to express it, but it will not work as a business if people are unwilling to pay you for the product or service.

For each home-based business concept, you must be aware of the following:

- So how are people willing to pay for my product or service?
- Can I make a decent living off of that?

Assume you want to start a creative business making homemade quilts with your sewing skills. However, you can only make two quilts per month due to the time commitment. You learn that people are willing to pay $300 for each quilt you make. This generates monthly revenue of $600 after deducting the costs of quilt production and advertising.

This may be enough if you want to earn a little extra money each month doing something you enjoy. However, if you want to make a living from your business, less than $600 per month will most likely be insufficient.

Most businesses require time to generate a profit. Take this into consideration, and plan ahead of time for a period when you don't expect your business to be profitable. Although, for your business to succeed, you must eventually meet your income targets consistently.

Determine your monthly minimum income requirements and only consider business ideas that have a real chance of generating that level of profit.

Chapter 2 | Create a Business Plan

Business plans are not only required for startups seeking a business loan. The primary reason for creating a business plan is to determine whether your idea has a chance of succeeding.

The Marketing Plan

The marketing strategy is at the heart of your business's rationale. Therefore, a home-based business owner must learn about the market to develop consistent sales growth. To demonstrate your comprehension, this section of your home-based business plan should attempt to answer several basic questions succinctly:

Who is your market?

Describe your typical customer's profile. The profile may include your customer's age, gender, family structure, income, location, and purchasing habits.

Describe your trading area geographically: (For example, county, state, national, etc.)

Economically, describe your trading area as follows: (Single-family, median income, number of children, etc.)

Who is your competition?

No home-based business exists in a vacuum. Learn about and respect your competitors. Make your marketing plans more specific. Determine direct competitors (both geographically and in terms of product lines) and those who are similar or marginally comparable. Begin by compiling a list of names, addresses, and products or services. Provide the following information about each of your competitors in a brief but concise manner:

1. Who are the people who are closest to you?
2. In what ways do their businesses resemble or compete with yours?
3. Do you have a distinct "niche"? Please describe it.
4. How will your service or product be superior to or more appealing than your competitors'?
5. Is their business expanding? Stable? Declining? Why?
6. What can be gained by observing their operations and speaking with current or former clients?
7. Will working from home give you a competitive advantage or disadvantage? Be truthful!

Remember that your company can become more profitable by adopting good competitive practices and avoiding their mistakes.

Check the standard characteristics like price, performance, durability, versatility, accuracy, ease of operation or use, ease of maintenance or repair, cost of installation, size or weight or color, appearance or styling, or packaging (you may want to add more from your knowledge of your field) and make an honest evaluation. Finally, indicate your potential and a total score on a scale of "0" (theirs is better than mine) to "10" (mine puts theirs to shame).

A Total Points rating of less than 60 indicates that you should reconsider the viability of your product and think about ways to improve it. Conversely, over 80 points indicate a significant competitive advantage.

- What share of the market are you planning to take?
- What are your pricing and sales terms?

The main consideration in pricing a product or service is the value that it represents to the customer. If your product is truly ahead of the competition on the previous checklist of features, you can command a premium price. If, on the other hand, that is a "me too" product, you may need to "buy" a piece of the market to gain a foothold before attempting to raise the price later. This is always dangerous and difficult. One rule will always apply: the market will ultimately determine the price. You will fail if your selling price exceeds your costs and expenses by the margin required to keep your business healthy. Understand your competitors' pricing policies. Send a friend to compare prices. Is there any discounting going on? What about special sales? Who are the price leaders? Make a couple of "blind" phone calls.

What is your sales plan?

Describe how you intend to sell, distribute, and service the products you intend to sell. Be as specific as possible. Some common practices are listed below:

Direct sales by telephone or in-person

Individual sales representatives who sell through party bookings, door to door, and distribution of call-back promotional campaigns have increased dramatically, implying that careful research is required to be profitable.

Mail Order

As more two-income families find less time to shop, specialized markets for leisure time or unique products have grown. Keep up to date on recent mail-order legislation and regulations.

Franchising

  a) You can either become a franchisee in someone else's franchise or start your franchise operation in which you sell tasks to specific territories or product lines to others. Each will necessitate additional legal, financial, and marketing research. (A free sample of a home-based business plan is available, as is a template for a home-based business plan.)

You could choose to work as a local or regional distributor for a variety of product lines.

What is your advertising plan?

As part of the overall business marketing strategy, each product or service will require its advertising strategy. Take some time to review a few basic assumptions before developing an advertising campaign for your business plan. Marketing is described as any paid, non-personal promotion that communicates with many potential customers simultaneously. Advertising's goal is to inform, persuade, and remind customers about your company's products or services. Every advertising activity should have a clear goal in mind. Common examples include:

- bringing in orders or contracts
- To publicize special events such as sales, business openings, and the introduction of new products.
- To submit requests for estimates or to have a sales representative contact you
- A specific goal at the outset could be to use special media to establish yourself even before you launch and to gather potential customer "feedback."
- One or more of the following may be included:
- Obtaining and distributing business cards to prospective clients
- Posting notices on free bulletin boards in supermarkets or office complexes in the area
- A phone survey of potential customers to inform them of your startup plans.

- To determine what types of advertising are appropriate and within company budget projections, you must carefully review your customer profile.
- Create a clear statement of advertising goals based on this review.

The fundamental criteria for selecting specific types of media will include brief answers to the following questions:

Trading Area - Do you intend to serve or sell to an industrial market, a national market, a local market, or a specialized market?

Customer Type - What does your prospective client read or listen to? Where? How frequently? What image does the media you're thinking about convey? Is it appropriate for your customer?

Budget Restrictions - What types of media will you be able to use if you have a limited budget? How can you properly spread your budget over a year to send a consistent, repetitive message? While you may need to invest more initially, a good long-term rule of thumb is that advertising should not properly exceed one or two percent of sales.

Continuity of Message - Where will the type of service, customer profile, and seasonal purchasing patterns influence your media selection and advertising frequency?

Past Performance - And what's the track record of the medium you're considering for your type of business? What tools do your competitors employ? What advice does your trade association have?

Management Plan

Who is going to do what? Include the following four basic sets of information:

- Provide a personal history of the principals and any related work, hobby, or volunteer experience (include formal resumes in Appendix).
- List and describe each person's specific duties and responsibilities.
- List each person's benefits and other forms of compensation.
- Identify additional professional resources available to the company: Accountant, lawyer, insurance broker, banker, and so on are some examples. Describe each's business relationship: "Accountant available on an as-needed part-time hourly basis; the initial agreement calls for service providers not to exceed x hours per month at $ xx. xx per hour." for example.

Begin with a simple organizational chart that lists specific tasks and shows who will do what, as indicated by arrows, workflow, and lines of responsibility and communication.

Detail a proposed work schedule by month and week for at least the first year. If any gaps in personnel skills have been identified, explain how you intend to close them through training, the purchase of outside services, or subcontracting. For assistance, contact the nearest state employment service office.

What is your banking plan?

What are the location and type of bank accounts that will be opened for the business? A word of caution: keep business and personal accounts separate. These vital records will be required in the future for tax and accounting purposes.

How Is Your Credit Rating?

This question may have several partial answers. However, everything will be crucial to the company's future. So, first and foremost, what is your personal debt-paying history?

To properly establish a credit rating, it is necessary to obtain and use credit from various businesses. Your rating will be determined by your track record of paying for goods and services by the agreed-upon terms. If you have a poor credit rating, talk to your lawyer, accountant, and banker about ways to improve it before applying for and being denied business credit.

The Financial Plan

The Financial Plan is the most important section of your Business Plan Document. In developing this section of the planning document, you will create critical schedules that will guide your company's financial health through the turbulent waters of the first year and beyond.

Before looking deeper into the particulars of development, a home-based work business financial plan, it is critical to understand that some basic accounting knowledge is required to manage your business effectively. If you're like most home business owners, you're likely to have a strong and abiding interest in the product or services you sell or intend to sell. You enjoy what you do, making it even more satisfying that you can make money doing it. Nothing is wrong with that. The belief that what you are doing or making is worthwhile is critical to success. Nonetheless, a coach who takes great pride in producing a winning team will rely heavily on someone keeping track of the wins and losses.

The business owner is no exception. Your product or service may benefit humanity for generations to come, but unless you have an unlimited bankroll, you will fail if you do not make a profit. If you do not know what's going on in your business, you won't ensure its profitability. Most home-based businesses will use the "cash" method of accounting, with a record-keeping system that may be nothing more than a carefully annotated checkbook in which all receipts and expenditures are recorded, supported by a few different types of original entry

If your business is more than a small supplement to your family's income, you'll need something more sophisticated. Stationery stores can sell you a variety of packaged small business accounting systems that include simple journals and ledgers as well as detailed instructions in easy-to-understand language.

If you believe your accounting knowledge is so rudimentary that you will require professional assistance to set up your accounting system, the classified section of your phone book can direct you to several small business services that provide a full range of accounting services. You can purchase as much as you require, ranging from a simple "peg-board" system to computerized accounting and monthly profitability consultation. Rates are properly reasonable for the services provided, and an investigative consultation is usually provided free of charge. Make some calls under the heading "Business Consultants." Make sure to tell them how big your company is so you can get to the ones who specialize in home-based operations. Many of them are home-based entrepreneurs themselves, so they understand what you're going through.

Let's begin by taking a look at the components of the company's financial plan.

The following are included in the Financial Plan:

1. **Financial Planning Assumptions** - These are brief descriptions of the conditions under which you intend to operate. These include market health, startup date, sales buildup ($), gross profit margin, required equipment, furniture, fixtures, payroll, and other key expenses impacting the financial plan.

2. **Operational Plan, Profit, and Loss Projection** - This is planned for the first year, divided into twelve months. It should serve as your first-year budget.
3. **Source of Funds Schedule** - This diagram depicts your capitalization funds' source(s) and how they will be properly distributed among your fixed assets and working capital.
4. **Pro Forma Balance Sheet** - The term "pro forma" refers to the fact that the balance sheet is prepared before rather than after the fact. This form displays the company's assets, liabilities, and equity. This will indicate how much investment the business will require and how much it will be used as working capital during its operation.
5. **Cash Flow Projection** - This forecasts cash flow into and out of your business over the year, allowing you to plan for staged purchases, high volume months, and slow periods.
6. **Creating the Profit and Loss Projection** - Create your Profit and Loss Projection using the form below.
7. **Profit and Loss Projection-** Every month, assess your company's profit or loss.
8. **Controllable expenses-** Operating supplies, gross wages, repairs and maintenance, advertising, car and delivery, bad debts, administrative and legal fees, and outside labor charges are all examples of controllable expenses.
9. **Fixed expenses-** Rent, utilities, insurance, taxes and licenses, interest, and depreciation are examples of fixed expenses.

10. **Source of Funds Schedule-** Make a list of all the assets you intend to use in your business, the amount of investment required for each, and the source of funds to capitalize them.

Indicate the number of months of useful life for depreciable fixed assets before leaving your Source of Funds Schedule. (In this case, the pickup truck, packaging machine, furniture, and office equipment are all depreciable.)

This information will be required to enter as monthly depreciation on your Profit and Loss Projection. In addition, the Balance Sheet will require all of the information from the Source of Funds Schedule.

Creating the Pro Forma Balance Sheet

Here's an example of a Balance Sheet. There are several variations of this form, and you should ask your banker for the form that the bank uses for small businesses. It will properly make it easier for them to assess the health of your company.

Even if you intend to postpone the purchase of some assets throughout the year for this pro forma Balance Sheet, properly assume that all assets will be provided at the time of startup.

Cash Flow Projection

A monthly Cash Flow Projection is an important subsidiary schedule to your financial plan. A prudent business management practice keeps no more money in the business than is required to run it and protect it from disaster. Having too much cash is rarely a problem in most small businesses. A Cash Flow Projection is created to inform management of the amount of cash that will be absorbed by the business's operations and compares it to the amount that will be available.

Is Additional Money needed?

Assume you've determined that your business plan necessitates more funding than sales can provide. What are you going to do?

What you do is determined by the circumstances. For example, your company may require bank credit to get through the lean months. This loan can be repaid during the high-volume sales months when expenses are significantly lower than sales. Sufficient working capital is required for success and survival.

A Final Word on your Home-Based Work Business Plan

You have properly invested a significant amount of time and effort in completing this worksheet. You should now have everything you need to create a prospectus for your business as simple or as complex as you want. More importantly, you've created the management tools that will help you succeed in your venture. You will be inundated with the details, problems, challenges, and joys of going it alone once the company opens its doors. It will be difficult to stay on course through the rough seas ahead, but don't forget your "chartbook," which will get you to "Port Profit." It should be a work in progress that you refer to regularly, massage, and revised to reflect your experience.

Begin a planning cycle that extends this first-year plan to three or five years in the future. It will be updated regularly. Set goals and stick to them. Your success is in your own hands. Excellent planning and execution!

Chapter 3 | Things to Consider Before You Start a Home Business

What is the ideal home-based business for you? First, you've listed your qualifications. Next, you've mentioned your passions. Next, you've described your family's ideal way of life. Finally, you've devised a business plan. Next, consider the following questions: Are there customers for my product or service? How do I know this? How will I track them down? What are my competitors' names? How much will I charge? How will I market my product? Finding answers to all these questions is the difficult and time-consuming homework that will help you determine your chances of success and whether you should pursue a more marketable idea.

What Is My Product?

The product you are offering is most likely the most crucial aspect of your business. Whether you decide to provide dog bathing services, design roll-top desks, accounting and teaching services, or car maintenance services, you must ensure that your customers know this.

The first step in starting a home business is deciding on a product. What do you have to offer? Next, write a brief, specific statement describing your product or service.

Developing a clear vision for a business concept is one of the most difficult aspects of starting a business. As you experiment with the market and put your skills to the test, your statement may change several times. For example, instead of displaying that you make toys, you could limit your product line to only making wooden dolls. Instead of writing software for small business needs, you could tap into a larger market and provide accounting package training to small business employees. Finally, examine how it feels to describe your product or service to family, friends, potential customers, and other business owners. Is your description concise and clear? Can you say it with assurance and zeal?

Who Will Buy It?

Answer the question, "Who will buy your product or service?" before developing and testing your home business idea. Make a list of potential customers: groups, individuals, population segments, or other businesses that require your product or service. For example, how will you quickly and cheaply find a market for fabric-covered lap boards for people who are confined to bed?

Through hospitals or home health care agencies? By displaying them as gift items in craft stores? In a mail-order catalog? Is there a market route that will reach out to children? Solicit the assistance of friends and colleagues in brainstorming all possible markets (customers) and uses for your product or service.

Who Is the Competition Home Based Business?

Your home-based business planning must also include a current analysis of your competition. Why? Because you must plan your market position or how you will fit into the market. Will your product or service be less expensive or more expensive than the major competitors'? Will it last longer? Will you be open at times when your competitors are closed? What advantages can you incorporate into your product or service that your competitors do not? Will you take on rush jobs?

When planning your business, look for a unique niche that will free you from stiff competition or make your product or service more valuable than others on the market. For example, if you intend to open a day-care center and discover that none in your area is open before school, an early opening may help your service compete. Likewise, if you discover that local caterers have overlooked the office party market, you could include a note about it in your brochure. The more information you have had about your competitors, the better you will decide how to position yourself properly in the market.

Advertisements in newspapers and trade magazines are also excellent sources of market information. To gather market and pricing data, consult the Chamber of Commerce, your county's economic development office, the Census Bureau, and professional and business organizations.

Where Are the Buyers? How Can I Find Them?

You'll learn where and how to find buyers as you become more familiar with the competition. Whatever type of home business you want to start, you'll need to conduct market research to find out if there are buyers for your idea, where they are, and how to find them. (You'll also be gathering pricing information in the process.)

Visit your local library to gather local and county statistics on the size and composition of your market. (While you're at it, get some books on marketing research, so you know what you're getting into.) Also, look for online and offline resources that may contain information about your product or service or the people who will use it.

After you have completed your marketing research, you will have

Identified your potential customers; learned everything you can about their habits, needs, preferences, and purchasing cycles; and decided how to reach them to generate sales.

How Much Shall I Charge

Four major factors will influence how much you charge for your product or service:

- your direct and indirect costs;
- the profit you hope to make;

- market research data on competitors' prices; and
- the market's urgency

There is rarely a single "correct" price, but rather a reasonable price range within which you should aim. Avoid the common blunder of many new business owners: charging too much or too little. Instead, use several approaches to arrive at a price and "test" it. For example, your price may be too high if your ego is too involved. On the other hand, if you think "this is just a little something I do in my spare time" or "anyone could do this," your price may be too low.

Here's a formula for determining a reasonable price. Before you make a final price decision, calculate it using the following methods:

Typical Pricing Formula

1. **Direct Material Costs**--Calculate the total cost of the raw materials required to create your item. Next, calculate the cost of a group of items and then divide the total cost by the number of items to determine the cost per item. Fine if you can quickly and easily determine the material cost of a single item. On the other hand, some items are produced in batches, and it is simpler to calculate an item cost by splitting the cost of a batch by the list of pieces eventually produced.
2. **Direct Labor Costs**--Calculate how much you pay your employees to produce the item (whether or not

you have employees now). Even if you are the sole manufacturer of the item, you must assign a wage figure. Divide the weekly salary you pay someone to produce the required number of items by the number of items. Add this figure to the total of Direct Material Costs.

Materials + Labor = $

3. **Overhead Expenses**--Rent, gas, and electricity, packing business phone calls and shipping supplies, delivery and freight charges, insurance, office supplies, postage, payroll taxes, cleaning, repairs, and maintenance are examples of these costs. The accuracy of your costing is dependent on estimating logical amounts for all expense categories. For example, if you work from home, calculate a portion of your total rent or mortgage payment or assign a reasonable, competitive rent figure for the same amount and type of space. Next, make a list of all overhead expenses and total them. Finally, subtract the total overhead figure from the number of items sold per month (or period you used above). The answer is your per-item overhead.

Overhead + Materials + Labor = Total Cost/Item

4. **Profit**--Include an amount related to the price of each item to ensure that you do not simply break even or pay the employees' wages. Check out what your competitors are charging. (Retailers typically charge

twice the wholesale price.) Charge a little if your product is superior to the competition. If your product is comparable, set a comparable price for it. Remember that you will receive the profit from each sale in addition to your salary. To get your total price per item, add the profit figure you chose to the total cost per item.

Profit + Total Cost/Item = Total Price/Item

Remember that the primary goal of running a business is to make a profit. Don't undersell your product or service because "I'd be baking cakes anyway," "I'm just getting started," or "I work from home." On the other hand, customers may be willing to pay a little more if you have a new, rare, handmade product or a personalized service.

Home Based Business Promotion

Promotion is a long-term strategy for informing potential customers about what you have to offer. Advertising is commonly regarded as the paid communication component of a promotion program. To create a comprehensive promotional campaign, you must first answer the following questions:

1. What image or message do I wish to convey?
2. What are the most effective media and activities for reaching out to potential customers?

3. How much time and money am I willing to put into the effort?

Create a long-term, consistent program for image enhancement and customer outreach. Your company's image should be reflected in your business card, logo, stationery, brochure, newsletter, phone answering service, signs, paid advertisements, and promotional activities.

Word-of-mouth recommendations from satisfied customers are the most effective form of advertising for any business. Consider which promotional tactics will help you gain the confidence and image you want: giving speeches and interviews (which are often effective for counselors, teachers, lawyers, and consultants), having an open house or holiday home sale, holiday recitals, or shows, free demonstrations, and samples.

A series of small ads may have a greater impact than a single large, splashy ad. So, instead of a one-time ad or event, run a campaign. If you properly hire a public relations firm, look for one that can provide you with personalized service and develop a comprehensive marketing strategy for you, rather than just a few advertisements. The plan also included market research, a profile of your intended audience, a part of the imaging system they recommend you project, written copy, and a list of media that are best for your type of service. As a new business owner, you will most likely decide to set aside a set amount of money per year or a percentage of past, projected sales for paid advertising.

You are the boss of your work-from-home business.

"Yesterday, I did not even know how to spell ENTREPRENEUR, and now I am one!" read a sign on a new business owner's desk. Now that you've decided to start a home-based business, you'll be responsible for all decisions, not just the ones you previously enjoyed, because they involved your area of expertise. You have over 21 years of experience as a consultant advising organizations on personnel matters, but do you know if it is advantageous to incorporate? You're an expert in word processing, but do you know how to set up an effective record-keeping and billing system? You are the boss now, and your home-based business's success depends on your management abilities.

Conclusion

If you have ever properly wanted to learn how to start a small business from home, now might be the time. Because of the global COVID-19 pandemic, more people than ever are working from home and starting their businesses.

Although starting a business from home has advantages, there is a lot to learn to be successful as with any business. In this guide, we'll walk you through everything you need to know to start a home business, step by step.

So, if you're wondering how to start a small business at home properly, you'll discover that the process necessitates planning, preparation, and documentation (and legal).

Although starting a business can be overwhelming, if you take things one step at a time, you'll properly find that the process becomes much more manageable. Furthermore, when you start and run a business from home, you don't have to worry about finding an office or retail space.

Visit And Buy the Other Books of This Author

Happy Saint Patrick's Day: Saint Patrick's Day Planner/Journal with 8.5x11 inches and 100 Pages

https://www.amazon.com/dp/B09BY841SZ

St. Patrick's Day: Saint Patrick's Day Planner/Journal with 8.5x11 inches and 100 Pages

https://www.amazon.com/dp/B09BY7XWGD

Happy Easter: Easter Egg Patterns Worksheet: 8.5x11 Inches 60 Pages

https://www.amazon.com/dp/B09BT2B6F3

Easter Hunt Activity Happy Easter: Easter Hunt Activity Journal | Notebook size 8.5x11 60 Pages

https://www.amazon.com/dp/B09BY7XWKL

Easter Day Spring Writing Assignment worksheet: Easter Day Spring Writing Assignment worksheet | 8.5x11 60 Pages | Spring Worksheet

https://www.amazon.com/dp/B09BY5HNVB

Cinco De Mayo: Large Updated Organizer with Daily Spreads For 2 Months with Cover Paperback https://www.amazon.com/dp/B09BY8178L

Taking full charge of your finance: Easy Guide to Personal Finance

https://www.amazon.com/Taking-full-charge-your-finance/dp/B099C8S85Z

Sure, Steps to Wealth Creation: How to Build Wealth from Nothing

https://www.amazon.com/Sure-Steps-Wealth-Creation-Nothing/dp/B099C3GNQH

All You Need to Know About Cryptocurrency: Understanding Risk and Reward in Investing

https://www.amazon.com/Need-Know-About-Cryptocurrency-Understanding/dp/B099C3GNML

Eliminating Your Debt in 12 (x) Easy Steps and Keep Them Off: A Practical Guide to Eliminating Your Debt Forever!

https://www.amazon.com/Eliminating-Your-Debt-Easy-Steps/dp/B099BZX4FX

NLP For Beginners

https://www.amazon.com/NLP-Beginners-RS-Johnson-ebook/dp/B098JBH28Q

Credit Repair Secrets

https://www.amazon.com/Credit-Repair-Secrets-RS-Johnson/dp/B098JH79X2

<-END->

www.ingramcontent.com/pod-product-compliance
Lightning Source LLC
Chambersburg PA
CBHW030039230526
45472CB00002B/591